FORGOTTEN RESPECT

Navigating a Multigenerational Workforce

Unlock the code for building and retaining teams working across five generations.

Dennis E. Gilbert

© 2015 Dennis E. Gilbert

All rights reserved. No part of this book may be used or reproduced in any manner whatsoever without written permission except in the case of brief quotations embodied in critical articles and reviews.

Published in the United States of America.

CreateSpace Independent Publishing Platform

North Charleston, South Carolina, United States

ISBN: 1515279464

ISBN-13: 978-1515279464

LCCN: 2015912291

Slow starts, setbacks, and failures: success stories are not about the people who went through them but rather about the people who grew through them.

~Dennis E. Gilbert

CONTENTS

	Preface	vii
	Acknowledgments	xi
1	Who Are We?	1
2	Not the Same	7
3	Communicating	21
4	Conflict Erupts	33
5	Feedback	43
6	Decision Style	53
7	Traditional Leaders	67
8	Boomer Leaders	73
9	Gen X Leaders	81
10	Millennial Leaders	87
11	Generation 9/11 Leaders	93
12	Respect	99
13	Building Strategy and Vision	111
	Index	123
	About the Author	135

PREFACE

Generational diversity is a constantly changing subject. Just three or four years ago, many experts would've agreed that only four generations exist in our workforce. Today, in 2015, many of those same experts would conclude that there are five. In another five or ten years, this may again fall to only four, or the popular wisdom that frames today's categories may shift.

This book consists primarily of my view of the generations in our workplace today. My views are a culmination of having lived for five decades and having been in the workforce for more than three of those, many as a formal leader and many as a business and workforce consultant. It is the result of my being the youngest sibling in my family and of my parents not only living through the Great Depression of the 1930s but also being more than thirty-five years old at the time of my birth. I sometimes joke that I grew up with old people, and now I am one of them.

Throughout this book I offer ideas, conclusions, and strong opinions. I provide illustrative examples in numerous places suggesting what a person from a specific generation may think or feel in response to workplace directives or communication. This disclaimer applies to the entire book: the illustrative examples may not be representative of every person in any particular generation, but they are provided as an example and, perhaps, a general characteristic.

I also ask you, the reader, many questions. Much of the work in this book is derived from my own personal readings, courses of study, and life experiences, and this work may include popular wisdom or argumentative positions. My hope is that this book will challenge you to think more about your interactions with everyone in the workplace and that you will do your part, no matter how big or how small, to create a stronger culture and greater success.

Frameworks for each generation are defined in the opening two chapters. I will state now that while there is much agreement formulated from various sources on the existing frameworks, there is often disagreement as well. Personally, I believe the last emerging generation, labeled here as generation 9/11, likely starts around 1990 instead of the mid 1990's, or even later. Much debate continues among experts on this emerging generation; my choice at this time is to lean towards many main stream viewpoints consistent with the mid-1990's time frame, but I offer that my position on this latest generation is still evolving, with more on this to come in future works.

Starting at the end of chapter 3, and located at the end of each chapter that follows, I have provided closing tips identified with the label "Across the Generations" inside a text box. While I determined this not appropriate or necessary for the first two chapters, I offer it as a chapter summary, as suggestions for forward thinking, or simply as helpful tips. Each "Across the Generations" section emphasizes commonalities, not differences, and is intended to help the reader develop a broader viewpoint.

Finally, I hope that you will find more commonalities with any generation that is different from your own. This book and many of our thoughts when interacting with others will quickly highlight our differences, but it is our commonalities that will help us discover—and never forget—respect.

ACKNOWLEDGMENTS

So much work goes into any book that I often undergo a moment of emotional tugging when I start to write something as brief as an acknowledgment.

I believe that everybody's life is rich as long as they live it. Because I have been on this journey for five decades, I can tell you that I've had some moments of brilliance and some moments that were not so brilliant. I'm grateful to all the people who have given me their time and energy and supported me through the ups and downs. I'm grateful for those who have offered their wisdom and suggestions and pushed me further with their questions.

This book is about workforce generations, but writing it has also refreshed my values and enhanced my respect for people of all ages. I offer my extended thanks and appreciation to each and every person I talked with about this book while writing it. There are many of you, and you, my dear, dear friends, have made a difference.

CHAPTER 1

WHO ARE WE?

Understanding today's generational definitions.

WHO ARE WE?

Generational diversity discussions come in many different forms. Often the first thought relates to age. In workplace circles, and in any polite circle, it is considered inappropriate to discuss age. Perhaps no three-letter word makes human resource professionals shudder more than the word *age*.

Defining who we are is much more challenging than stating the number of years we have been alive. Defining our level of emotional maturity and how we interact with others may be much more subjective than objective.

Workplace generations have some common labels and definitions, and still there are sometimes variances from expert to expert as each considers placing a frame around blocks of years that represent a generation. Typically,

WHO ARE WE?

generations are defined by significant changes in world socioeconomic trends, technology shifts, and even war.

I'm not sure if it is safe or appropriate to suggest that experts agree on anything, but many experts seem to follow a fairly consistent pattern of agreement on at least some of the generational definitions. Many may still argue that workplace cultures, businesses, industrial sectors, and physical locations such as rural versus urban can also represent some specific challenges or frameworks for groups.

Another somewhat interesting truth about commonplace generational definitions is that the length of a generation, typically represented in years, also varies considerably. On the outset, some think of generations as those typically defined by our family tree, perhaps lasting from grandparent to parent to children and covering many years, maybe even a century or more. These thoughts need to be dismissed as we consider workplace generational diversity because

FORGOTTEN RESPECT

a typical generation by workforce standards is much shorter.

At the year of this writing, 2015, and for consideration during the scope of this book, consider that there are at least five generations currently existing in our workforce.

They are the following:

Traditionals

—Born between 1930 and 1945

Baby Boomers

—Born between 1946 and 1964

Generation X

—Born between 1965 and 1976

Millennials

—Born between 1977 and 1994

Generation 9/11

—Born after 1994

WHO ARE WE?

Of course, some may challenge the labels, as well as the time frames, but this framework does align closely, if not exactly, with many commonplace US definitions. Other countries that study or examine workplace trends related to employee age may have a broader or narrower framework.

Helping to illustrate how our year of birth may shape our views or define our generation, consider this simple example. Ask a person of each generation just listed to tell you something about the following people:

John Travolta

Ralph Waite

William Shatner

O. J. Simpson

Ron Howard

Some will recall John Travolta as Vinnie Barbarino from the hit television show in the 1970s *Welcome Back Kotter*. Some will recall William Shatner as Caption Kirk from the original *Star Trek* series, which aired in the late 1960s, while others may know him from today's Priceline television commercials. Some may recall Ron Howard as Opie from *The Andy Griffith Show*, as Richie from *Happy Days*, or as an American film director and producer today.

Imagine all of our life's experiences, values, and socioeconomic trends coming together in the workplace as we work in groups, make decisions, or lead teams. All of this experience doesn't necessarily make anyone wrong or right, just different. Yet our differences are not what I want you to consider the most, because differences draw a line and tend to keep us apart. What I believe is most valuable is what we have in common.

Are there other considerations for framing generational diversity? Is the diversity consideration as unique as each organizational culture? Perhaps the most important factor for consideration is that some reasonable framework be defined that allows for the generalization of helping individuals and teams succeed.

CHAPTER 2

NOT THE SAME

It is not about differences, it is about commonalities.

NOT THE SAME

Any conversation about generational diversity also likely includes one about differences. During seminars or keynote speeches, I often express to groups that the focus should be not on differences but on commonalities. Considering that, it would seem remiss if we didn't briefly explore some of the characteristics behind the framework for labeling the generations. I want to provide some definitions.

TRADITIONALS
(Born: 1930–1945)

While not many of this generation may still be in the workplace today, their legend lives on.

NOT THE SAME

By definition they lived during, or very close to, the Great Depression of the 1930s and up to and including World War II. This time of economic collapse, hardship, and turmoil certainly shaped many lives.

Today, those who represent this group have a view of life that is likely much different from that of the millennials or generation 9/11. In the workplace, they may have a feeling that they no longer belong—or worse, that the younger generations want them gone. As if that isn't already enough, they may also feel some resentment about working. While some may do it because of boredom or the need for activity, many are likely doing it because of financial need—a need they didn't plan for but now face.

This generation either is interested in or completely dislikes technology. Computers, electronic devices, pocket telephones, or touch keypads and screens may be either loved or hated. What may make this concept worse is feeling pressured or pushed into adapting to the technology when they really don't see the need to.

Loyalty is an admired strength of most of this group. During much of their careers, the mindset of thankfulness for a family-sustaining wage for many years was held in high appreciation. CEOs didn't change often, product life cycles were longer, and family values were likely different. Much of today's workforce population would label this group as very loyal.

Generalized, this group is also very disciplined. They learned to seek stability, and once they found it, they cherished it, respected it, and were committed to it. Day-to-day responsibilities were task centric, and their commitment to employers promised to yield continued opportunity, a stability indicator that was desired by both employee and employer. Financial security likely mattered, but that security was most likely measured through consistency rather than entitlement or fast-tracked success.

BABY BOOMERS

(Born: 1946–1964)

Often cited as the largest generation—thus the name baby boomers—this generation also typically is representative of supervisors, managers, and other authority or knowledge-oriented job titles. Because they have likely been in the workforce for some time, they offer a vast array of experiences. While some believe this generation is the most educated, others suggest that postsecondary education was still not mainstream during the time many of them entered the workforce. Still others contend that regardless of their educational background, this generation believes most strongly in postsecondary education.

The baby boomer generation often attempts to place a value on workplace contributions based on hours of effort. In other words, they believe long hours somehow measure or equate to output. While of course this could be true, for most this concept does not appeal to the notion of productivity. Productivity should be measured by accomplishments across time, not time spent equating to accomplishment. For example, one widget per hour, or eight widgets per day, does not mean that spending ten hours per day will improve the one-widget-per-hour metric. In fact, it could become worse or less, dropping to 0.90 per hour if only nine widgets were produced in ten hours.

Boomers often are also viewed as a generation that likes to stick to what works. While this may suggest resistance to change, it may also hint at the notion that decisions are based on long-term observations and outcomes. However, we live in a world of constant change, and these long-term outcomes may not be the best method for tomorrow's solutions.

NOT THE SAME

GENERATION X

(Born: 1965–1976)

Somewhat in contrast to the baby boomer generation, this group is often known for their desire to mix things up. Repetition equals boredom, and boredom means disengagement. What may be a blind spot for some, but certainly not all of this generation, is the lack of connection with persistence to achieve success. As a result, their critics may suggest that much of this generation represents slackers. This label is certainly not highly regarded or respected.

Generation X may be considered to have a very low tolerance for what they regard as poor management. In the face of poor management, they simply want to go a different direction and mix it up, and they are committed more to the ideology of change than earlier generations tend to be.

Being regarded as credible by this group often requires proving yourself. Credibility and even integrity are examined from words, actions, and behaviors; they are typically not assumed or given. In other words, you are not worthy until you prove yourself.

Some suggest this generation embraces the concept of work hard and play hard. Still others suggest a different idiom: work hard, play harder. Some believe this generation started to shift the idea that long hours equate to levels of contribution. Many cite this group as the generation that embraces management by objective.

They may be viewed as very self-sufficient, quick starters, and fast learners, and they admire clear and up-front communication. They want to see management philosophies that are farsighted, encouraging, and accepting. They may label themselves as having a stronger interest in change than the one to whom they report to in the workplace—likely a baby boomer.

NOT THE SAME

MILLENNIALS

(Born: 1977–1994)

Enter the age of the socially conscious. Many would agree that this group represents those who have been shaped by large-scale topics such as global warming, urban sprawl, and the fate of the social security program. Some would offer that members of this group are more willing to spend frivolously, expect entitlements, and blame others for their own shortcomings. However, experts have mixed opinions about those areas, and as with generalities across all workplace generations, these qualities are certainly not representative of everyone.

Being more youthful than some of the generations mentioned earlier, this segment is very high energy. They are mostly eager, and they love anything that integrates technology. While many people in this generation are concerned about long-term governmental policy, such as the social security system, just as many are not that interested in wages versus quality of life. In other words, they like flexibility. More work or overtime programs are not particularly attractive to many among this generation. They would sooner be given more opportunity for days off or what we often label "comp time."

Love of technology abounds in this group. They grew up with technology, and it has become an integral part of how they navigate life. This often leaves them believing they are truly capable of multitasking, and they may be known to encourage an environment that allows web surfing during business meetings, strategy sessions at the coffee shop, and headphones and music while they work.

Certainly, this is not being mentioned as right or wrong but rather as a point of interest, especially as we consider not what is different across the generations but what each generation may have in common.

NOT THE SAME

GENERATION 9/11

(Born: After 1994)

One common characteristic of this group is that they have generally known only a time of turmoil and war. While some may argue this point, they also have known only a relatively weak economy. Of course, there have been ups and downs, and who to blame is not relevant or destined for this book.

Likely, the most significant shift is caused by the event that creates this generation's name, the September 11, 2001, tragedy. They have largely heard and accepted that the world is uncertain, loyalty has diminished, and their values and beliefs are not highly respected. Simply put, they see very little certainty in their futures. As a result, the things that cause fear and panic in some of the earlier generations simply do not seem to faze a generation that expects it; this is the only way of life they know.

Long-term commitments may be hard for this group to accept or deliver. Higher divorce rates among their parents or grandparents make them somewhat split on relationships: some insist on them, while others don't believe in nearly any long-term commitments.

Some observers may suggest that this group is more entitlement oriented and requires a lot of feedback in the workplace, perhaps a societal condition stimulated by the "every kid gets a trophy" philosophy. Different from earlier generations, they may expect things like their parents paying for their postsecondary education and their first car, and they may live in their parents' home for much longer periods of time than earlier generations did. Some of this may be by choice; some may be a condition of a chronically weak economy or perhaps just a continuation of a societal shift.

This generation is nearly completely dependent on technology. Some suggest, in an exaggerated fashion, that this group has never touched a hardcover book. They may not understand the Dewey Decimal System or know the difference between a table of contents and an

NOT THE SAME

index, and their research is predominantly influenced by online materials. Certainly, I'm not suggesting that any of that is either good or bad—just that it may be different from other generations.

FORGOTTEN RESPECT

CHAPTER 3
COMMUNICATING

More communication does not always mean better communication.

COMMUNICATING

Everyone recognizes, if asked—and sometimes if not asked—that communication in our lives and at our workplaces has a significant impact on the outcomes of relationships, productivity, and outputs. One reason for communication breakdowns is that many people launch into their best guess at a solution to a problem without really understanding or considering the problem's root cause. A common example of this is an organization's leaders believing that more communication is the answer. Of course, more communication may help, but this solution fails to regard some of the other possible root causes of communication breakdowns.

Meeting after meeting, e-mail after e-mail, and a growing carbon copy (CC) list is not necessarily the solution. Many people also report that such an approach potentially weakens the communication process because recipients become more inclined to tune out verbal communication and to delete, skim, or completely ignore e-mails.

If the solution is not more communication, should we consider another look at root causes? Yes, we should. Factors to consider would include an awareness of the need to communicate, reduction or elimination of fears associated with communicating, trust issues, and consideration of how recipients may perceive the communication. We all know that perception is reality.

Since this book is not intended to specifically examine awareness, fears, or trust, let's look a little deeper at perceptions of information as they relate to communicating across the generations. Are the listening skills of a generation X worker different from those of a baby boomer? Do millennials process information differently than traditionals do? Are barriers and filters different from generation to generation?

FORGOTTEN RESPECT

Consider this: a baby boomer supervisor says the following in a team meeting:

"We have to pick up the pace during the next two weeks. We are at the end of the second quarter of the fiscal year, and we are slightly behind our target. Does anyone have any thoughts on what we can do to improve our chances of making our goal?"

Now consider what the various generations may hear, think, or perceive from this message, such as the following:

Traditionals:

"If those younger workers would just quit screwing around…"

Baby Boomers:

"Yes, what is wrong with everyone else? Let's get the pace going."

COMMUNICATING

Generation X:

"Doing this month in and month out is boring. Can't we mix things up?"

Millennials:

"The system for processing our work flow is dated. We need more technology."

Generation 9/11:

"We'll never be able to accomplish those goals doing it the way they did it twenty years ago."

    Of course, this is just an illustrative example, and anyone from any generation could easily argue that these reactions are not representative of what he or she would do or think. Others could argue for stereotyping, listening bias (or perhaps writer bias), or some other position, but let's just consider for a moment that these are possible reactions. How would they affect the outcomes of the conversation? How would they change what each employee would suggest or do to pick up the pace? Would they pick up the pace?

What if we changed the generation of the supervisor?

Consider a millennial supervisor who is saying the exact same message:

"We have to pick up the pace during the next two weeks. We are at the end of the second quarter of the fiscal year, and we are slightly behind our target. Does anyone have any thoughts on what we can do to improve our chances of making our goal?"

What do the various generations hear? Their thoughts may be the following:

Traditionals:

"They want us gone. They believe we are slowing them down. Not everything is done through technology."

COMMUNICATING

Baby Boomers:

"OK, hotshot. Why don't you tell us how to do it, then?"

Generation X:

"Wow, give them a title, and they let it go to their heads."

Millennials:

"Finally someone has said it. Now let's make the changes necessary to improve productivity."

Generation 9/11:

"I'm not saying anything. I know those older workers don't like it that someone younger is in charge."

FORGOTTEN RESPECT

Again, this proposed communication is just an illustration of how various generations may perceive the communication. What is worse may be how they openly react to it. While this is a simplistic example, it does help set the stage for additional consideration.

As people, we tend to be information processors. Additionally, when we don't understand, we seek ways to understand. Sometimes this means we fill in the blanks. We hear or listen as someone speaks, and when we don't completely understand, we supply our own interpretation. Often, this is a leading cause of miscommunication. The multigenerational aspect increases the level of challenge.

Consider this: The owner of a business, a traditional, delivers a message to the management team. He closes with this:

"I'm glad everyone has been working so hard to meet the recent surge of customer orders. If this continues, we'll have to make some changes."

COMMUNICATING

How this may be interpreted:

Traditionals:

"There he goes again. He'll never actually hire more people."

Baby Boomers:

"Dang it, there goes our overtime. I was counting on the extra income."

Generation X:

"What does that mean? Does he think we can't handle it?"

Millennial:

"If we would throw away the chalkboard and abacus, the improved productivity would solve this problem."

FORGOTTEN RESPECT

Generation 9/11:

"I wonder if there is a YouTube video on how to manage this?"

All of this, of course, still holds my earlier disclaimer. This is not representative of everyone in any particular generation. It is offered to provoke additional thought as you consider communicating with others in the workplace, and more specifically a multigenerational workforce.

COMMUNICATING

ACROSS THE GENERATIONS

1. **More communication is not necessarily better communication.** While every generation might occasionally feel that insufficient or not the right communication is occurring, it is the quality and not the quantity or volume that sets good communication apart from bad.

2. **Trust is always a factor in every workplace generation; that means it is a commonality.** Perhaps nothing affects communication more than trust does. It takes time to build it; be patient, and don't underestimate its value.

3. **Each generation has its own unique framework and will listen and communicate through filters.** Don't try to change someone else; change the way you respond and interact to make your communication clearer.

FORGOTTEN RESPECT

CHAPTER 4
CONFLICT ERUPTS

Not all conflict is bad.

CONFLICT ERUPTS

At least two important factors are closely associated with conflict. One is our fear associated with potentially starting a conflict, and the second is effective management of conflict to keep it from becoming harmful. During seminars, I often suggest to participants that conflict is a natural part of people working together and that not all conflict is bad. Often, people label conflict as negative, harmful, or simply bad. I suggest that conflict becomes bad only when it is mismanaged.

FEAR

Let's start at the beginning with how fear affects our ability to communicate and connect across various workplace generations. Fear may cause us to simply not communicate. Of course, remember that silence itself may be sending a message.

Employees who lack trust in their organization, peers, or supervisor may often withhold information. They make a small mistake, but they don't trust others' reactions to it, so they try to hide it, cover it up, or minimize the significance of the error in their minds. They also may try to minimize it in the minds of those who noticed or witnessed the error.

Another great example is employees fearing the feedback process or simply the nature of upsetting another employee. Of course most, but not all, employees do not enjoy the idea of upsetting others. Feedback, discussed in another chapter in this book, often provides a great example of people avoiding a potential conflict. This assumes, of course, that the feedback is something related to performance improvement and not kudos.

The fear of conflict needs to be managed. We have to be able to accurately assess conflict across what I often refer to as the conflict continuum. On one end of the continuum, we have avoidance. On the other end, we have confrontation. In the middle, we have diffusion. We want to try to balance our approach to conflict, striving to process it somewhere near the middle and not at either end.

HARMFUL

Conflict becomes harmful when it is not managed effectively. Avoiding a conflict situation completely will typically worsen the outcome, either because of continued occurrences of the problem or through the subject matter festering and building into something even more significant. Either case would be considered mismanaged.

Consider an employee making an error. Let's assume he breaks a long-standing process (way of doing things) or tries to cut corners on a product or service to save expenses. If the employee is not made aware of this mistake or error in judgment, he may simply continue to do it over and over again. The short-term costs of managing this situation (potential conflict) are far lower than the long-term costs of inappropriately managing it or choosing to try to avoid it altogether.

New or different ideas for process improvements, cost savings, or improved customer satisfaction may have employees facing a potential conflict. All of these circumstances should be viewed as a natural part of conflict, and when managed correctly, they don't have to be harmful.

GENERATIONS

Do generational differences affect the nature of managing conflict? What about generational commonalities? It would seem that greater focus on commonalities would help to minimize potentially harmful conflict situations. So often, though, the first words we use relate to differences, not commonalities. Needless to say, there are differences and there are commonalities, and both make a difference for managing conflict across the generations.

If you subscribe to the idea that conflict does occur between workplace generations, then you may want to ask what causes this conflict. Conflict is going to occur anytime you work with other people, whether they are of the same generation or of different generations. So another question to consider is this: is conflict more predominant when working with people across generations or when working with people within the same generation?

You could probably build a case for the idea that conflict is more predominant when working across the generations, but I believe what is more important than whether conflict is more predominant or has increased is to develop a deeper consideration for what may be causing this conflict.

Let's consider an example. A baby boomer supervisor offers the following at a Monday morning staff meeting:

CONFLICT ERUPTS

"This is a big week for us. Meeting our customer goals will be challenging, and I'm expecting everyone to put in some extra effort this week. I'm confident that by Friday we'll all feel great about what we've accomplished."

Now, how might this be perceived across various generations? Here are some examples:

Traditionals:

"Great. I know we've got this. What are we waiting for?"

Baby Boomers:

"We've done this before; we'll do it again. The overtime will be great."

Generation X:

"Well, I know some of the team will put in the effort, but I'm not sure about everyone."

FORGOTTEN RESPECT

Millennials:

"As long as everyone is up for the challenge of multitasking, this will be a breeze."

Generation 9/11:

"I'm not sure if this is possible, but I hope we get it done. Friday is my half-birthday, and I don't want to be messing around here, being late, or whatever."

Once again, this is just an illustration, and some of the reactions may be exaggerated a bit to help demonstrate differences. For example, traditionals and baby boomers may be more focused on the task, while millennials and generation 9/11 may be more focused on getting the work done and allowing play time to begin. Many would agree that it is not uncommon for the millennial and generation 9/11 generations not only to be interested in social responsibility but also to have a better work-life balance. This is

CONFLICT ERUPTS

something that other generations could benefit from. Of course, often the lack of balance for them is self-inflicted.

Could generational conflict be the result of different goals and objectives and not differences in social values? Likely, it is some of both. Let's face it: younger workers likely do not have the same goals and objectives as a person nearing retirement has. However, at the same time, social values may also be different. A traditional or baby boomer may not expect much fuss about his or her birthday, whereas, as illustrated earlier, generation 9/11 has initiated the concept of half-birthdays. To clarify, a half-birthday is celebrated every six months, or once per year, and a birthday is also celebrated once per year. Earlier generations would probably offer, "So you have two birthday celebrations per year? You're spoiled." And with that, the conflict begins.

FORGOTTEN RESPECT

ACROSS THE GENERATIONS

1. **Avoidance is as problematic as being too aggressive.** Ask questions of others to gain understanding of specific interests or to clarify positions. Think collaboration.

2. **Conflict doesn't know generational boundaries.** Conflict is typical for groups of any generation; all generations have this in common.

3. **Different doesn't mean better or worse.** In conflict, a different idea is often managed as the wrong idea. The common ground should be inclusion not exclusion. Build on others' ideas to create synergy.

CHAPTER 5

FEEDBACK

Feedback, lots of feedback.

FEEDBACK

Performance evaluations tend to make people nervous. As soon as you start a conversation about feedback in the workplace, many people start to picture themselves sitting across the table from their boss, nervously waiting to hear the good, the bad, and the ugly that occurred during the past year.

While this may, in fact, be a feedback exchange, it is really not representative of what this chapter is about. The purpose of this chapter is to encourage feedback, not just at an annual or semiannual performance review but more frequently and perhaps less formally. Feedback, when properly managed, can propel teams to reach higher, dream bigger, and achieve more.

The feedback exchange in organizations is not limited to supervisor to direct report. Feedback should be intentional and should occur often. It is appropriate to communicate feedback from direct report to supervisor, peer-to-peer, and of course supervisor to direct report. We may also have feedback exchanges with customers and vendors. Simply put, feedback is a communication process intended to strengthen relationships and improve performance.

TYPES OF FEEDBACK

When asked about the types of feedback exchanges we could experience in the workplace, people often suggest that there are two distinct types. First, there is positive feedback, which is given when we do a great job. It entails receiving kudos, or people saying we've done nice work. Second, there is negative feedback, which would typically be described as anything that is not positive. One might describe it as "what I did wrong."

This very mind-set of two types of feedback, one being positive and one being negative, may be the first idea that needs to be changed. During seminars on this topic, I like to suggest that there may be three types of feedback: (1) positive, (2) performance improvement, and (3) mismanaged, with mismanaged feedback most often characterized as negative. Performance improvement feedback is not, and should not, be negative.

GENERATIONAL FEEDBACK

Feedback may be one of many examples in which there is more at work in people than just age differences. Truly, societal shifts have caused differences. Consider the often-mentioned idea that "every kid gets a trophy." The latter part of the millennial generation and nearly all of generation 9/11 experienced this concept.

Somewhere along the way, society started to believe that participation in youth team sports and some other activities warranted every child participant walking away with a trophy. While opinions may differ on what sparked this or what the desired outcome was, I think most people would tell you that it was intended to boost children's confidence and balance out the kudos across the entire team. Yet even this concept has consequences or at least sparks some debate.

Consider that youth positioned in these later generations have different expectations about participation. First, they expect lots of kudos along the way. They may even expect kudos for moderate or average performance, or perhaps even for bad performance. They expect feedback often, and they are shocked when limited or no feedback occurs. Second, they expect a reward at the end of a time line or milestone. This may be a monetary reward, a "pizza party," or some other significant celebration.

In some circles, this is also labeled as a sense of entitlement. To others, the idea of entitlement goes deeper. It crosses generational boundaries and may be much more related to social demographic values than to certain generations. Again, though, arguments exist for many different sides.

TIMELINESS OF FEEDBACK

Popular wisdom may suggest that we should never let issues fester. We hear about this in management circles, we're taught this in conflict management, and we know it as a common truth. Of course, the idea of issues festering draws us more toward conflict management and not specifically feedback. We also quickly recognize that the feedback process has the potential to require conflict management skills, but then again that may depend on the nature of the feedback, kudos, or performance improvement.

Mismanaged feedback is untimely. Feedback in the heat of the moment may not always be the most constructive, either from a delivery standpoint or from a listener's standpoint. At the same time, feedback delivered too late has less value and may be prone to causing future problems. Also, unfortunately, if it is performance improvement related, more of the "wrong" behavior or actions can occur while someone hesitates and procrastinates over the best time or place for delivery. Like many things in life, this requires some good judgment to find the right balance.

I have not specifically mentioned or described feedback from supervisor to direct report; however, I must stress that this is often where our minds take us. It is what we've been taught. Feedback is not only about supervisor to direct report. If you're thinking that way, stop.

QUANTITY

Yes, feedback may occasionally face quantity considerations. Too much feedback, for example, consistently saying "nice job," may start to feel like sarcasm or diminish its value and meaning. On the flip side, too little feedback also becomes problematic. While I hate to generalize, my belief is that one of the many challenges facing generational issues is that it is just that, generalized. To clarify, what I am suggesting is that many different personalities, social norms, and values exist across all generations, so to cite a particular reference with a guarantee of a specific

FORGOTTEN RESPECT

outcome within a specific generation would likely be both careless and inappropriate.

Generally speaking, then, the generations that have more recently entered our workforce are likely to expect more frequent communication compared to the generations that have come before them. Baby boomers may often suggest that no feedback means you're doing OK, but for the millennial or generation 9/11 employee, no feedback, or very limited feedback, may have them in a high-anxiety frenzy.

Largely because of different societal standards, the post-World War II boomers are not so expectant of feedback, at least not compared to the "every kid gets a trophy" standards that many people of the millennial and generation 9/11 generations may hold. We know that expectations condition our perception of outcomes, and being more forthcoming with feedback, and doing it often, will likely result in stronger relationships. Keep in mind, though, that this feedback should be both congratulatory

FEEDBACK

and performance-improvement oriented, but never negative, or mismanaged.

ACROSS THE GENERATIONS

1. **Well-managed feedback improves performance.** Negative feedback means mismanaged feedback. Your goal should be to help the recipient succeed. Every generation needs well-managed feedback.

2. **Timing is critical.** Feedback delivered too early or too late doesn't have the most effective impact. Timeliness is not an issue of generation; it is an issue for discipline and commitment to positive performance improvement.

3. **The feedback process is not one way.** Feedback is two-way communication and should reach across all generations as well as organizational levels.

CHAPTER 6
DECISION STYLE

Considering decision style across the generations, what is your style?

DECISION STYLE

We all make decisions, right? Every day we make choices and take actions that result in outcomes. In simplest terms, we decide what to wear, what to eat, and even to some extent what we'll do. We also interact with other people. We decide what we'll say during those interactions, what we'll do, and how we'll move forward. Decisions surround us. Do we all have the same decision-making style? Are our decisions based on experiences? How do our experiences shape our choices?

Most decisions we make are based on some framework. This framework may be established or created based on our life experiences, and it may be supplemented by certain stereotypes, biases, or learned (right or wrong) responses of what we believe to be ethical. In still other cases,

DECISION STYLE

digging deeper, people may challenge our behavior or decision-making style due to factors such as human need (survival), addictions, and risk or consequences. Do you agree that these all may be factors?

Whether you agreed or not, you just made a decision, and most likely your framework, as just illustrated, guided that decision. Therefore, what is likely valuable for us to consider is how the various generations that we've defined make choices or decisions. How do we eliminate or take into consideration other internal or external influences that may affect decision-making style? Are there other factors involved? Factors such as addiction, peer pressure, or group think?

Let's consider a scenario. A generation X supervisor leads a meeting with her staff. She offers the following for discussion during the meeting:

"We are not achieving our sales goals. What is worse is that we can barely keep up with the demand in our current model, and recently I know we've come up short on meeting some of the quality expectations of our most valuable customers. I'm opening up the discussion for thoughts or ideas on what we could do to improve. What are your thoughts?"

The team may be thinking the following:

Traditionals:

"We're spending too much money on things that aren't necessary. If we had a little more cost control, we wouldn't have such lofty sales goals."

Baby Boomers:

"The whole team should be putting in more time, including the boss. If you want to fix this, we have to work harder."

Generation X:

"Have we ever accomplished those goals? Maybe they are too lofty."

DECISION STYLE

Millennials:

"The whole team is burned out. We've been putting in all this extra time and effort for nothing. If some of these people could accomplish more and maybe multitask for a change, we would have this problem under control."

Generation 9/11:

"This just seems like we are on a path to nowhere. I'm not sure what else we can do. I want to Google this right now, but using my phone in the meeting will make the boss angry."

How do the different generational experiences shape our thoughts, strategic thinking, and decision-making style? Consider simply that many traditionals, on one end of the generational continuum, may never even consider "Googling" it, and yet generation 9/11, on the other end of that continuum, may think of that first. Who has the best method? Which will result in better decisions or outcomes?

Nearly any generation could make an argument for their style or their way of thinking. Many times in our workplace, we struggle with the concept of timeliness, and thus, another factor enters this picture. Whose decision style is more beneficial, the person who decides quickly or the one who is more calculated? Which style weighs risk more effectively?

When we consider the cost of procrastination and constant consideration of the data and facts, or collecting more of both, what is the cost? Many apply a cliché to this issue, calling it analysis paralysis. Yet we also have to respect the idea that a decision to do nothing is, in fact, still a decision.

So many questions, yet perhaps not many answers. Is it reasonable to suspect that, as with other elements we've explored, generational differences and commonalities affect our decision-making processes? I offer the notion that the answer is yes. Even in the simplistic example in this chapter, we could quickly determine that what our experiences are to date may have some effect on the decisions we make. In group settings, group dynamics may also create—or fail to create—reasonable choices. What we may desire are good, quick, and high-quality decisions.

Of course even these ideas make some assumptions. One assumption is that quick decisions are better than long, drawn-out decisions, and another is that quality may be an element of timeliness. The idea of what is "good," of course, is very subjective unless we put some measurements or metrics to the test. Quality, too, may be very subjective unless it is measured.

Is critical thinking part of decision making? I believe absolutely, yes. Do our experiences drive our critical eye? Can critical-thinking skills be taught? I believe yes, and yes. Critical thinking often develops or does not develop through our consideration of things like data anchoring or our ability to see patterns in data or facts.

FORGOTTEN RESPECT

ANCHORING

Anchoring occurs when we hear or notice some measurement or data element. As thinking people, we draw close to that anchor point or element, and it shapes all of our thinking.

Imagine that I told you I sat close by a drive-through restaurant during the busy noon hour. I say I observed about sixty cars pass through that drive-through during that timeframe, and then I ask you how many cars actually passed through. What is your best guess? Many people (but not everyone) would likely give a number close to my estimate. They may suggest fifty-five, or they may think my number is low and say seventy-two or some other ballpark number.

In another scenario, I could offer that I sat close to a drive-through restaurant during the busy noon hour and observed around 150 cars pass through the drive through. Then I could ask, "What is your best guess on the actual number?" Once again, many people would likely target a number close to or within reason of the 150.

DECISION STYLE

This is known as data anchoring. We base our thoughts and our decisions on supplied data, all the while assuming that there is accuracy in that data. Now, let's take a moment and apply this in our workplace. Many people in the workplace begin to make decisions and shape their thinking by data anchoring. The employee from the traditional generation who is asked about how to create more throughput or increase outputs may anchor to the idea of, "We need more employees," because from her or his experience, headcount was typically added to increase output. A millennial generation employee may think it is all tied to technology. Yes, there is a difference in thinking, but what is the commonality here? The commonality may be that both are connecting their thoughts or decision-making style to what they know or best understand, which may be their experiences. This may cause them to anchor to those exact experiences.

PATTERNS

Patterns may also shape our thought process, decision-making style, and, of course, outputs. Patterns of data may cause us to search for like patterns again and again, which scientifically may draw us toward some conclusion. Patterns may not always mean we're seeing the same thing over and over again. We may be seeing the same thing, but differently. Palindromes create a perfect example of how patterns can shape our choices. Palindromes are the same data observed, read, or understood the same way when presented both forward and backward.

Here is an example. Consider the following list of dates:

June 11, 2016

June 12, 2016

June 13, 2016

June 14, 2016

June 15, 2016

DECISION STYLE

Are these palindromes? Some would say no, but others may quickly say yes. What if we present the data differently?

Consider this representation of the same dates:

> 6/11/16
>
> 6/12/16
>
> 6/13/16
>
> 6/14/16
>
> 6/15/16

Is this a palindrome? Do you see it?

Let's take one more step:

> 61116
>
> 61216
>
> 61316
>
> 61416
>
> 61516

FORGOTTEN RESPECT

This is a palindrome. The data has the same representation when presented both forward and backward. This is true not only with numbers but also with words and even phrases. How about the words kayak, radar, or rotator? They have the same spelling read forward and backward.

How does this apply in our workplace? Are there ties to generational diversity?

A few of my thoughts are, yes, because our ability to see patterns may help us draw conclusions or find possible solutions to problems by recognizing the pattern. Failure to see the pattern may result in doing more of the same. So, for example, if we have the ability to see patterns, we may be able to do something some people struggle with, like reverse engineering.

Let's say we start something, hit a peak, and then decline. When we see that same pattern of start, peak, and decline over and over again, we may be able to reason that we have to do something different to prolong the desired peak.

DECISION STYLE

It may be hard, or considered a stretch, to draw on the idea that palindromic thinking or patterns are in any way related to the generations in our workforce today, yet at the same time, some would argue that technology itself can lead to more opportunity to discover such patterns.

Take, for example, modern scientific work in areas such as DNA sequencing, the search and discovery of the god particle, and our quest to understand more and more about the physics at work in our universe. Much of this work is based on accumulated knowledge during the past century or two. Each successive generation of thinking builds on the last, and in some cases, they go in completely different directions. Without hesitation, I would suggest that these outcomes are shaped by the ability to see, understand, and either change or adapt to patterns. All of these are the result of a decision.

FORGOTTEN RESPECT

ACROSS THE GENERATIONS

1. **Everyone makes decisions; style is more about perceived risk than about generations.** Perception of risk may either expand or limit choices. This is true for everyone regardless of life experience or generation.

2. **Past experiences drive choices, but more experience doesn't always mean better decisions.** Data anchoring and patterns are more likely to affect decision quality than experience is. Every generation has values and beliefs relational to their experiences, not to their age.

3. **Time is a constant regardless of generation.** Some will feel decisions are taking too long, while others believe they are made too quickly; neither of those thoughts is generation specific.

CHAPTER 7

TRADITIONAL LEADERS

It all starts here.

TRADITIONAL LEADERS

Among the workforce population, traditionals represent one of the smaller groups. According to the definition, they would be at least seventy years old at the time of this writing. I meet these folks, quite often in fact, because they are often small business presidents, CEOs, and owners. It is not uncommon to hear that more and more people are working past sixty or sixty-five, and in somewhat of a contrast, some are retiring from a job earlier in life, collecting a pension, and then reentering the workforce in some other capacity or sector. Overall, many agree—although it hasn't been verified empirically—that we are seeing older workers in our workforce.

Traditionals have seen a lot. While it may be somewhat unlikely that those born during the

TRADITIONAL LEADERS

Great Depression of the 1930s are in the workforce, those who by age fit this generation were likely born during the World War II era. What may be more or at least equally important is that their parents were Great Depression survivors. The label of traditional may seem fitting, or it may seem out of place, but this group represents what by current standards would be labeled old school.

Some rugged, some eloquent, but all hard charging and likely somewhat conservative because of their Great Depression values, a traditional as a leader is likely very people oriented, at least compared with being technology oriented. While they may question the loyalty of other generations, they hope that their employees are an investment in their team and business. They've lived with values of loyalty, integrity, and discipline, and they expect the same in return. This is often their measurement of respect, and they make every attempt to lead by example.

Often they may be known to be very kind, generous, and supportive of the more recent generations when they themselves feel well respected. They are interested in leaving behind a legacy and are eager to help and support those who seek their approval or advice. Keep in mind that they've lived most of their life in a different time, socially. By today's standards, male traditionals may seem somewhat gender biased and may stereotype women as suited for administrative work only. Female leaders may be eager to support more modern viewpoints on gender in the workplace. It is likely that neither males nor females in this generation will walk a very broad gender line; they must overcome bias if they hope for a gender-neutral workplace.

Traditionals as leaders are most likely not resentful about still being in the workforce. While they may be there based on some needs, they are also likely enjoying their time spent there. Some more recent generations may refer to them as "lifers"—a label worthy of only those who may have a lifelong struggle with the work-life balance or those who remain in a single organization for a long period.

TRADITIONAL LEADERS

Even though they may be workplace leaders, they may also feel somewhat alienated or out of touch socially. While this varies greatly from person to person, if they haven't really adapted to modern technology, they perhaps fail to understand why people are always messing with their cell phones. Those who are more open may see the technology in action and may start to welcome it. Still others will likely never understand what all the hype is about.

What does respect look like to a traditional? What are their values and beliefs? Whether you are or aren't one, how will you work with the traditional leader?

FORGOTTEN RESPECT

ACROSS THE GENERATIONS

1. **Engage with people.** Traditionals are much more likely to engage through person-to-person contact than through technology. Traditional leaders want to interact with, get to know, and connect with you interpersonally. They typically welcome (productive) team meetings and opportunities for group interaction.

2. **Illustrate loyalty.** Holding loyalty as a significant value, the traditional leader will most likely desire your demonstration of loyalty and commitment. Talking about job hopping, selling out a coworker, or breaches in integrity are conversations that won't last long.

3. **Engage face-to-face.** If you are in close physical proximity, go see them. If you are not close, telephone them. Save e-mail for very short updates or for your third choice to communicate. Not close but have an airplane? You know what to do.

CHAPTER 8

BOOMER LEADERS

You've been around for a while.

BOOMER LEADERS

Many believe that the baby boomer generation represents the biggest group of formal leaders. Born before 1965, they represent people who today are approximately fifty-one years old or older. Since most have been in the workforce for some time, much of this sector has been elevated to supervisory or managerial roles. In the United States (and not limited to only the United States), some of these people may be on their second official career. Perhaps they have retired and are now receiving a pension from a previous employer.

One common area of distinct difference between this generation and those that come after it is that they often believe that hours "served" or "put in" to the job somehow demonstrate or measure their effort or commitment. This is in sharp contrast to more recent generations, who may pride themselves on completion of objectives and their work-life balance rather than trying to prove commitment through long hours. Right or wrong, if your boss (aka leader) believes long hours prove your commitment, you may have to consider how that affects you. Some will consider how they can work toward changing that perception, if it exists.

This generation also served as the front-runner to advanced education as a core value. This has continued in the many decades that followed, with the idea that if you don't have "your card punched," you don't get in the door. This of course means that you have obtained some level of postsecondary education. Most commonly it represents having obtained a bachelor's degree. However, many of this generation went very far with high school education, certificate programs, and associate degrees. Your position on postsecondary education may differ, regardless of generation.

FORGOTTEN RESPECT

On the subject of education, some very well-known boomers showed that postsecondary education doesn't matter. People like Bill Gates (born in 1955), dropped out of Harvard and created the now infamous Microsoft Corporation. Michael Dell (born in 1965, right on the edge of the boomer generation) dropped out of the University of Texas at Austin to create Dell Computer. There are others, and some would claim they are exceptional people by IQ, SAT scores, or other measurement criteria. I mention all of this in the hope that all readers of this book, whether highly educated or not, are not being judgmental of one another.

Baby boomers are often regarded as one of the generations resistant to change. I know of no empirical evidence to prove that boomers are any more or less change resistant than other generations. In cases of boomers being change resistant to the point of holding it as a value, they are most likely not individuals having successful careers in leadership roles today. I would offer that change resistance is representative of a commonality across all generations rather than isolated in only one or two generations. Those seeking to find fault or place blame for a company or people failing to change may be quick to pass judgment on a generation different from their own.

ACROSS THE GENERATIONS

1. **Put in your time, lots of time.** If you want to gain their respect, show them that you aren't opposed to coming in early, staying late, or working weekends. It doesn't have to be fifty-two weeks per year, but illustrate your willingness to put in the time when necessary.

2. **Demonstrate learning.** College or no college, illustrate your interest in advancing the team through books, seminars, or videos. They know that learning improves performance. They have learned much during their time, mostly through old school methods, which they thoroughly believe in—it's tested, and has passed.

3. **Discuss options and choices.** Boomer leaders are change leaders. This sometimes may feel different from boomers who are not in a leadership role, since the general population of boomers is sometimes thought to be change resistant.

BOOMER LEADERS

Present facts, avoid opinions, and be willing to explore discussions of options or different directions.

FORGOTTEN RESPECT

CHAPTER 9

GEN X LEADERS

Growth is not just a number.

GEN X LEADERS

This is perhaps the biggest generational diversity sector of those moving into supervisory or more senior supervisory roles. This group may represent the present-day force of many organizations. They have likely been in the workplace for a number of years, so they bring great value in knowledge, strength, and hopefully leadership. Much of this group has experienced the rise of revolving door leaders. This means simply that as things transitioned from the 1980s into the 1990s and then onward into the 2000s, it perhaps seemed almost trendy to have a CEO for anywhere from eighteen to thirty-six months, and then he or she would move on. Sometimes it was by choice, and sometimes it was not, but regardless, the age of highly tenured CEOs seemed to evaporate.

Generation X employees have been known to have rather low tolerance for poor management, perhaps incentivized by the wave of shorter-term executive leadership. Much of this group, or at least those rising to the leadership challenge, will be sure they work both smart and hard to prove their worthiness and value. The desire to not be just another "revolving door" victim, or as they may say, "empty suit," means they wish to earn your respect, not assume that it comes with the title. Since they may believe you have to prove yourself, the great ones will likely walk the talk.

Interestingly, some of the earlier generations have occasionally referred to this group as slackers. It would seem realistic that a shift from *long hours means hard work* to *meeting objectives means hard work done smart* could provoke a viewpoint of slacker from those who have come before them. Adding to that is the popular 1990s concept of work hard, play hard, and you have the formula for drama.

My experience has been that this group also began to lead the charge of repetition is boring, so let's mix it up a bit. Perhaps they should get

FORGOTTEN RESPECT

some credit for pursuing more job rotation concepts, a trend that those representing the earlier years of this group may have experienced in full force. Both services- and production-oriented organizations were trying to improve both worker loyalty and efficiencies by mixing things up whenever and wherever possible. Not that the concept is good or bad, and it still is commonplace discussion or execution in many sectors. It may also go by another name: cross-training.

While every generation likely believes organization politics are problematic, this generation was perhaps the first to start doing something about it. Often, their careers have been shaped by learning to be self-sufficient and less dependent. Born before the more entitlement-oriented generations, leaders of this generational sector may seem matter of fact, with clear and upfront communication—perhaps blunt and less graceful with their words. Expect the generation X leader to not tiptoe around problems and issues from a communication perspective but rather tackle them straight on.

GEN X LEADERS

This more direct approach sometimes causes discomfort with both the generations before them and those that came after them. While earlier generations may have produced leaders with a more authoritarian approach, those formal leaders likely reacted accordingly because they were often raised on the do-it-or-die, my-way-or-the-highway philosophy of supervision. Generations that come after generation X may also be shocked because some of the people in those generations have been shaped by a kinder, gentler approach, with a "Make it OK for me" perspective.

Make no mistake about this generation. If they are in a leadership role or capacity, they will likely desire that you follow them, and they will work to obtain your support. But they will never expect that just because they have a formal position, you automatically will. At the same time, they will also exhibit low tolerance for incompetence or political nonsense. Given that in most cases they have another ten, twenty, or even thirty years to flex their muscles, how might they shape the organization of the future?

FORGOTTEN RESPECT

ACROSS THE GENERATIONS

1. **Be appropriately assertive.** There is no point in wasting any time with fluffy conversation unless you want to impress them with a new advertising campaign.

2. **Become comfortable with giving and receiving direct communication.** Anything else would be a waste of time, and it may be considered disrespectful for you to think they can't handle tactful and direct approaches to communication.

3. **Respect is earned, not given.** They may be somewhat undecided about what long term means to them and may want to prove their ability to stick things out and never quit or back down. Those who honor and exemplify this spirit may be granted their highest respect.

CHAPTER 10

MILLENNIAL LEADERS

No worries start something new.

MILLENNIAL LEADERS

Representing some of the newer leaders, this group will most likely lead with the intent and consideration of social values and technology. They have heard time and time again that there will not be any social security program for them when they retire, and as they look at their grandparents, or perhaps their great-grandparents, they are unsure how they will survive.

As leaders, they want to be socially responsible, and they want to build everything they do around technology. Both desires are respectable and appropriate, but neither is necessarily valued highly by earlier generations.

How will the millennial leader manage a traditional or baby boomer employee? Will there be friction and inconsistent ideologies on both extremes? Is it challenging when you are younger and managing older employees? What if you are older and have to report to someone half your age?

One good trait of millennials is that they tend to be open-minded. They are not so fixed in their ways, and they have grown up in an era in which it seems that everything changes. If they are thirty years of age (born in 1985), consider what they have experienced since being a teen. The past fifteen years, one-half of their life, they have experienced the 9/11 tragedy, US presidents with completely different ideologies, and economic conditions that many view as substandard.

Millennial leaders have high energy; they also are interested in doing as much as possible through technology. Consider that many of them grew up with the emergence of video games as traditional board games declined; they still had house phones and landlines but most likely use only a cell phone today. Family divorce rates continued to climb during much of their childhood, and as such it is likely that 40 percent or more of this generation came from mixed families.

They know a different world, see it through a different lens, and want to change it for the better. Some may hold some resentment against generations that have come before them, believing that they had it easier, took advantage of it, and as a result, the fallout is left for millennials and generation 9/11 to fix. What could we expect them to think? If they watch many popular news stations on television, they will likely find support for this belief.

Social media minded, they might get most of their support from social media channels. I don't believe this is good or bad, but it is different from what some of the generations that have come before them experienced. Most who are active in this new age media would likely agree that there are pros and cons to social media. So the net result is that the influence is different.

Earlier generations may say that leaders in this generation are influenced by a sense of entitlement, especially those representing the latter half of this group. How would this influence their leadership presence? Some might believe that they are fast trackers, those who desire to rise up in organizations quickly—faster than the average employee. They might also suggest that this group commands pay that is too high too quickly, expecting to achieve the same accomplishments as their elders in a very short period.

This group may represent a social shift in leadership style. As each day, month, and year go by, and as earlier generations and ideologies exit the workforce, this group will be shaping the new age. How will their values change leadership? For today, how will every workplace generation adapt to changing values?

FORGOTTEN RESPECT

ACROSS THE GENERATIONS

1. **Display social interests and values.** Leading is important and work is work, but what are you doing about social values? Show you care, are concerned, and most importantly, are willing to get involved.

2. **Think across the boundaries.** Open-mindedness is a value and belief system for millennial leaders. Be willing to stretch across formal frameworks and leap hurdles in the spirit of moral or social responsibility.

3. **Solve it with technology.** Whatever stands in the way of progress, solve it with technology and let go of any workflow traditions that don't include state-of-the-art approaches.

CHAPTER 11
GENERATION 9/11 LEADERS

The latest model is always the best, or is it?

GENERATION 9/11 LEADERS

Generation 9/11 leaders do exist. In fact, they're everywhere. While often cited as one of the most unemployed sectors, there are still plenty of leaders out there. While this sector probably has fewer in leadership roles (without fact checking), there are still plenty of them. There could be a number of associate degree graduates in this sector moving quickly into leadership roles; however, many still attending college or others who may not be enrolled in postsecondary education are still effectively supervising not only employees in their same generation, but those of the generations who have come before.

Many would argue that very limited experience puts this generation at a disadvantage not only for employment but also, especially, for a leadership role. Let's not forget, though, that leadership qualities may be developed at a fairly young age and that many persons in this generation have already proven their leadership skills. Of course, knowledge from textbooks, classroom projects, athletics, or other extracurricular leadership roles may not be exactly the same as being a supervisor in a very fast-paced and generationally diverse organization, but nonetheless some of this generation may have already been in the workforce for three or more years. That could represent, depending on their exact age, somewhere close to 20 percent of their lives.

What may be most important to consider, different from some of the earlier generations, is that this group has predominately known only a time of war and a weak economy. Some may dispute this idea, depending on what you consider a time of war and the definition of a weak economy, but I believe many would agree. The 9/11 tragedy shaped a different set of beliefs for this generation compared to that of the earliest generations that are still in the workforce.

FORGOTTEN RESPECT

At dinner tables, if what many would call a traditional dinner table existed for this group, they may have overheard and felt the struggles and pain of a very uncertain future. They may have also moved frequently, experienced mixed (divorced) families, and developed what some would term a sense of entitlement. Because of so much uncertainty, they may fear the future. As current workplace leaders, their high energy, social concerns, and use of technology may have them taking very little for granted and being focused more on short-term gains than on long-term investments. I'm not talking specifically about finance, although it would also apply.

Definitions of both short-term and long-term commitments may be different from those of previous generations. A baby boomer leader may view long-term commitment as twenty years or more, whereas a generation 9/11 leader may consider two or three years a long-term commitment. This is critical from the leadership point of view and is especially relevant from the standpoint that while the definitions may be different, the basis of the idea remains the same.

GENERATION 9/11 LEADERS

Much like respect or success, persons of all generations may define them differently, but one thing all generations likely have in common is that keeping promises or commitments represents something they desire.

Generation 9/11 leaders most likely wow coworkers or those who are direct reports from generation X or earlier with their technology skills. They know only technology. Their social awareness includes viewing it predominately through a technology lens. How will this generation of emerging leaders shape the workplace of today? It's likely that in only a few more years, the traditional generation will no longer exist in the workplace, or only in very rare situations. What will represent the next generation of leaders? How will the social climate, economy, technology, and global relations shape future leadership roles?

ACROSS THE GENERATIONS

1. **Demonstrate that you value knowledge.** They realize their experiences are not as vast as those of individuals in the generations before them, so to them knowledge—not experience—is the focal point.

2. **Use analogies in complex situations.** This group consists of sharp, fast learners. While their time in the workforce may be considered short, they've likely led in childhood sports, interests groups, or other young adult activities. Connect the dots across the generations with analogies that everyone understands. Don't forget they have a few for you too.

3. **If it's not technology, it may not matter.** All that they know is technology. Join them or get left behind.

CHAPTER 12

RESPECT

You may be nothing without respect.

RESPECT

Differences, differences, differences are mostly what we talk about when it comes to working in a multigenerational organization. Perhaps this is because it just feels natural to point out how someone is different from us. When comparing various generations, we tend to see the differences first—or perhaps worse, we see only the differences. Creating more workplace harmony, effectively communicating across the generations, and having respect for one another is critical for success. Why, then, does our human nature tend to focus on differences? Is it human nature or more of a learned behavior? Why not focus more on what we have in common?

Here are just a few thoughts that may speak about some of our differences:

RESPECT

Traditionals:

"Why do they eat out for lunch every day?"

Baby Boomers:

"Headphone, earbuds, or whatever you call them—they are clearly not appropriate on the job."

Generation X:

"Management isn't dealing with the problem performers, and I'm growing tired of doing the same old things."

Millennials:

"I really want to just work through my lunch break and leave an hour early each day."

FORGOTTEN RESPECT

Generation 9/11:

"We need more BYOD (bring your own device) meetings. It is much more effective when we just Google for solutions during the meeting."

Certainly this is very generalized and simplified, but it may help to further illustrate how we tend to point out differences rather than commonalities. Let's consider those same thoughts, except this time through the lens of searching for commonalities:

Traditionals:

"Lunch hours are important. I think it is best that everyone takes a break."

Baby Boomers:

"I don't understand the whole earbuds thing, but I guess if there aren't any safety issues and they are thorough and accurate in their work, what does it matter?"

Generation X:

"I guess I don't always agree with what my boss says or does, but I know we are all in this together, and I can live with that."

Millennials:

"I would sooner just have a quick snack, work through lunch, and leave early, but I guess if everyone had the same idea, we wouldn't be able to keep our normal business hours."

Generation 9/11:

"I think old-school meetings all the time are plenty boring, but I guess I can live without looking at my phone or notebook for an hour."

FORGOTTEN RESPECT

Once again, these are generalized and certainly not applicable to all situations or generations, but there is a slight difference in the thought process in this scenario. Some may suggest that it is a more positive approach, and that is probably true, but it is also more respectful. It sets an expectation or tone that while we may be different, we all should be considerate of others, recognizing that our way may not work for everyone. This approach is more respectful.

There is much more to consider. I'll often ask participants in seminars about both trust and respect. I may ask, "What breaks down trust?" or "What makes an environment lack respect?" Answers vary, but on the topic of respect, participants sometimes offer a time when someone made them feel devalued, a time when someone else took the credit for their work, or perhaps a time when they failed to listen to or consider another person's point of view or idea. Still others may describe with great detail and emotion a specific scenario that made them feel small.

RESPECT

Is there a pattern in this popular data? The pattern I see is that much of our consideration for respect, or a lack of it, centers on communication. Perhaps a think-before-you-speak habit should form, or when emotions are high and you're preparing an e-mail, a friend or colleague should review your words before you accidentally make a big mistake. In still other cases, sometimes we may have to trade popularity for respect. Perhaps withholding a joke or standing tough on a position may not be popular with everyone.

If you believe successful relationships in your workplace are based on being liked, ask yourself to think again. Being liked is very important. You probably won't succeed if you are outwardly despised, but at the same time you will definitely not please everyone, and when you can't please everyone, at least position yourself and your actions for the highest respect. Respect is not synonymous with being liked.

One noteworthy additional consideration is that a quick check on thesaurus.com indicates

FORGOTTEN RESPECT

that fear is a synonym for respect. People may be driven by fear, but when fear is used as a tool against them or as a method to provide motivation, it will likely be at the sacrifice of respect. Yes, of course, fear will motivate people, and it will even motivate some without significant consequence, but consider that traditionals may respond differently to fear than millennials or generation 9/11 employees do.

Personally, I always offer my opinions against fear as a motivator. It lacks the inspiration that is required for long-term achievement, it creates an "us" against "them" climate, and it breaks down loyalty and commitment. If that isn't enough, I also strongly suggest that it creates "paycheck only" employees. When they feel you don't respect them or care about them, then they in turn don't care about you or your company. They just want to put in their time and collect a paycheck.

Consider some of the following commonplace management phrases:

RESPECT

"If we don't change this, we'll all be looking for jobs."

"I don't even want to think about what will happen if we don't hit our sales goal this month."

"I know one thing: if we don't hit our quarterly goal, no one is getting a bonus."

Just harmless and normal workplace incentives to achieve? Some would say yes. Others may say, "Well, I didn't mean it to seem so harsh." Those simple phrases, perhaps taken for granted as normal workplace communication, could be the start of what propels a team to lose interest, lack commitment, and disengage. Are they motivational? Perhaps, yes, but are they inspirational? I would suggest absolutely not.

There are some who may suggest this is the way business is done. In today's world, I would say that in most cases, organizations that lead with this approach experience much higher absenteeism, turnover, and even theft.

You may ask, why theft? The answer is simple: Some develop the mind-set that you are shortchanging them, and they're going to make up the difference by taking something they want or need. This could be a material object or product, or it could simply be a resource, such as time. Employees who feel that the organization owes them are much less likely to uphold the integrity an owner or leadership team would expect.

What does all of this mean? It means that organizations that desire a multigenerational workforce that can discover synergy, harmony, and success should start with evaluating their level of respect across all generational sectors, all organizational levels, and throughout every employee team.

RESPECT

ACROSS THE GENERATIONS

1. **Always think before you speak to any generation, including your own.** Keep in mind that when you feel threatened or under pressure, your internal fuse will be shorter.

2. **Fear forms a connection to problems; inspiration connects to goals.** Avoid communication that enlists fear as a motivator. United groups are respected groups. Consciously or subconsciously creating a divide across any of the generations through fear will always be counterproductive and will feel disrespectful.

3. **Revert to mission.** Always connect every employee to the mission. When everyone understands their role and how their efforts contribute to the bottom line, there is a lot less room for drama or disrespect.

FORGOTTEN RESPECT

CHAPTER 13

BUILDING STRATEGY AND VISION

The success of a great organization starts with a good plan.

BUILDING STRATEGY AND VISION

Hopefully without argument, organizations would benefit tremendously from a very diverse multigenerational workforce. Even in organizations that focus on different ends of the generational continuum, there is likely value in having employees across the entire plain. Why in some cases, then, do organizations struggle to acquire, build, and retain a healthy multigenerational team?

We should remove the easy conclusions first. In certain geographic areas, the demographics may not support a wide range of generationally diverse teams—perhaps more common in rural communities than in metropolitan areas. In other instances, the size of the workforce for that organization may not really support having a wide, multigenerational team. In other words, of course it is more challenging for a ten-employee

BUILDING STRATEGY AND VISION

organization to hire a diverse set of workers than it is for a five hundred-employee organization to do the same. These are fairly straightforward and easily recognized issues.

In my experience, there are several problematic areas for organizations endeavoring to have a diverse generational team.

- They have a great mix of generations, but the generations don't work well together, resulting in higher-than-desirable employee turnover.
- They have trouble attracting certain generational sectors; especially those they feel are the most desirable for their organization.
- They discover that some generational sectors are attracted easily but are difficult to retain. They view the organization as a stepping-stone.

If you find yourself concerned about one or more of these three areas, you are certainly not alone. Organizational culture or the mission and vision of the organization will likely have a lot to do with any of these three areas. So will how your organization responds to or positions itself to adapt to social trends. You certainly cannot discount other factors such as wages and benefits, location, and community reputation.

Each organization will find people who need a job, want a job, and simply are happy with a paycheck. They'll also find those who are highly energized, have lofty goals, and are looking for a stepping-stone. In addition, they'll find those who may lack confidence or credibility and who view themselves as lucky to be employed. Should I continue? None of these probably represent the most desirable long-term, high-output, low-maintenance, and team-oriented workforce, regardless of their generational sector.

I suspect some of you will argue with this. Some of you will say you want people who are just happy to come on board and do a good day's work for an honest wage. Yes, we need some of those, but not by obtaining employees with low motivation or energy for the organization's purpose or those with conflicting values. And

BUILDING STRATEGY AND VISION

certainly not by obtaining employees with the mind-set of "you don't care about me and I don't care about you; we're both in this (organization and employee) just for the money." If this is the type of team you or your organization desires, you probably aren't reading this book, or you'll stop reading here.

What do many organizations do? Exactly what you would tell your best friend never to do in life: settle. Settle for whatever you can get. Of course, there are gray areas, geographic areas with less-than-desirable demographics, and so on. The key then, or so it would seem, is like a hand in a game of cards: make the most of what you've got. This is where vision, strategy, and culture play an enormous role.

Let's troubleshoot.

If you have a great mix of multigenerational employees, but the employees don't seem to get along well, how would we solve that problem? Answers may vary, but of course we should first discover the root cause. Likely, there is something in the culture of the organization or leadership that promotes or accepts this behavior. It could be factors commonly related to communication, such as trust, listening skills, and feedback, and all of these may have close ties to respect. Too much drama and too little trust and respect will promote this outcome. Organizations that have not created and intentionally worked hard to promote a sense of purpose will easily fall victim to these circumstances. In addition to a lack of purpose, confusion about the sense of purpose is problematic.

If you have trouble attracting certain generational sectors, you may have to honestly assess the values of being an employee at your company compared with socioeconomic trends. Manufacturing jobs or jobs requiring hard physical labor, such as construction trades, energy sectors, lumber harvesting, or farming, have a stereotype of being hard and sometimes undesirable work. At the same time, they may also be considered jobs that should be filled by the later generations rather than the earlier generations. Chances are good that two things will help: emphasizing the sense of purpose and highlighting the rewards. If the sense of purpose is not respectful or is low integrity and the reward system is not family sustaining, an organization will struggle with onboarding. Community reputation and social trends also remain problematic.

Organizations that onboard easily but are viewed as a stepping-stone may have completely different problems. Likely they are reputable and socially respected, with competitive starting wages, but they lack incentives or opportunities for advancement or are viewed as a low-end player in a specific industry. This may be common in the financial sector and can be especially problematic in banking. For example, obtaining a first-time job as a bank teller may appear respectful and come with high integrity. Long term, this job may not be desirable, but it may look good on a résumé if you are pursuing any job in the financial sector. Jobs related to commercial loans, real estate mortgages, investing, or even accounting fields could view these early career jobs, such as that of a bank teller, as a stepping-stone.

FORGOTTEN RESPECT

Each organization may have a different philosophy on how to manage this. Some will view it as the nature of the business and plan accordingly, and others will closely measure the cost of onboarding and attempt to create a purpose with career paths for all employees. I'm certainly not suggesting which way is the best, but if you value retention, the latter would seem much more appropriate.

I've touched on only three areas; they are: 1) a great mix of employees, but they don't get along well; 2) trouble attracting certain generational sectors; or 3) organizations with many positions that are viewed only as stepping stones and employees don't stay. There are likely others, and of course there are those that have a blending of problematic multigenerational issues. The solution for all three may vary, based on many factors that could include short-term and long-term strategy, workforce demographics, economic conditions, rural versus metropolitan location, and competing organizations.

BUILDING STRATEGY AND VISION

The vision and culture that each organization represents, which really means how the organization is perceived or its reputation, will greatly relate to multigenerational success. Creating a vision that is consistent with its mission, core values, and beliefs will go a long way toward having a harmonized multigenerational experience.

A well-respected organization will always perform better.

ACROSS THE GENERATIONS

1. **Never settle.** A multigenerational workforce strategy that is compromised is a strategy that will fail. This is not the same as a fluid strategy or changing to a different strategy. One that breaks its own rules will never succeed.

2. **Have a specific purpose.** Dogs do tricks for a reward; people are not dogs. People want the reward, sure, but they become connected to the organization only through a sense of purpose.

3. **Never confuse purpose with a paycheck.** Sure, monetary rewards are important, and they'll definitely keep people coming back, but it is inappropriate to assume money is the same as a sense of purpose. If it is, or if it becomes that, people will only be committed to the highest bidder. In this case, the bidding will occur often.

INDEX

INDEX

A

accomplishment · 12
achievement · 106
addiction · 55
advancement · 117
advice · 70
agreement · 3
anchor · 60, 61
Anchoring · 60
anxiety · 50
appreciation · xi, 10
argue · 3, 17, 25, 65, 94, 114
attracting · 113, 116, 118
avoid
  avoiding · 35
awareness · 23, 97

B

baby boomers · 11, 40
balance · 36, 41, 47, 49
behavior · 48, 55, 100, 116
behaviors · 14
beneficial · 58
benefits · 114
bidder · 120
birthday · 41
boredom · 9, 13
boss · 44, 56, 57, 75, 103
brilliance · xi
build · 31, 38, 88, 112

C

career paths · 118
celebration · 47
century · 3, 65
CEO · 82
CEOs · 10, 68, 82
certificate programs · 75
challenges · 3, 49
childhood · 89, 98
children · 3, 47
choices · 54, 55, 59, 62, 66, 78
coffee shop · 16

INDEX

colleague · 105
college · 78, 94
commitment · 10, 52, 72, 75, 96, 106, 107
commonalities · ix, x, 7, 8, 37, 58, 102
commonality · 31, 61, 76
communication · viii, 14, 21, 22, 23, 28, 31, 45, 50, 52, 84, 86, 105, 107, 109, 116
community · 114
company · 77, 106, 116
competitive · 117
conclusions · viii, 64, 112
confidence · 47, 114
conflict · 33, 34, 35, 36, 37, 38, 41, 42, 48
conflict management · 48
confrontation · 36
congratulatory · 50
considerate · 104

consideration · 4, 6, 23, 28, 38, 55, 58, 59, 88, 105
consultant · vii, 135
continuum · 36, 57, 112
contributions · 11
conversation · 8, 26, 44, 86
credible · 13
critical · ii, 52, 59, 96, 100
critical thinking · 59
cross-training · 84
culture · viii, 6, 113, 115, 119
customers · 45, 56

D

data · 58, 59, 60, 61, 62, 63, 64, 105
data anchoring · 59, 61
decades · vii, xi, 75
decisions · 6, 12, 54, 55, 58, 59, 61, 66
decline · 64

INDEX

definitions · 1, 2, 3, 5, 8, 96
demographic · 47
demographics · 112, 115, 118
demonstrate · 40, 74
Depression · 69
desirable · 113, 114, 115, 117
desire · 13, 59, 72, 83, 85, 91, 97, 108
despised · 105
devalued · 104
Dewey · 18
differences · ix, x, 6, 7, 8, 37, 40, 41, 46, 58, 100, 102
dinner · 96
direct report · 44, 49
direct reports · 97
discipline · 52, 69
disengage · 107
disengagement · 13
diverse · 95, 112, 113
divorce · 17, 89

E

economic conditions · 89, 118
educated · 11, 76
education · 11, 18, 75, 76, 94, 135
elders · 91
eliminate · 55
eloquent · 69
e-mail · 22, 72, 105
emotions · 105
employees · 35, 37, 61, 69, 82, 89, 106, 112, 114, 115, 118
Employees · 35, 108
encourage · 16, 44
engineering · 64
enjoy
  enjoyment · 35
entitlement · 10, 18, 47, 84, 90, 96
entitlements · 15
environment · 16, 104
examples · viii, 39, 46
expenses · 36
expert

INDEX

experts · vii, 3, 15

F

facts · 58, 59, 79
Failure · 64
families
  family · 90, 96
fast learners · 14, 98
fast trackers · 91
fear · 17, 34, 35, 96, 106, 109
feedback · 18, 35, 43, 44, 45, 47, 48, 49, 50, 52, 116
Female · 70
finance · 96
financial · 9, 117
Financial security · 10
fiscal year · 24, 26
flexibility · 16
focus · 8, 37, 100, 112
forget · x, 94, 98
framework · 5, 6, 8, 31, 54, 55
Framework
  frameworks · viii

friend · 105, 115
future · 48, 85, 96, 97

G

gender biased · 70
generalized · 49, 102, 104
generation 9/11 · 9, 40, 41, 46, 50, 57, 90, 96, 106
Generation X
  gen x · 4, 13, 25, 27, 29, 39, 56, 82, 101, 103
generations
  generational · i, vii, xi, 2, 3, 4, 8, 9, 13, 15, 16, 17, 18, 19, 23, 24, 26, 28, 34, 38, 39, 40, 41, 42, 47, 49, 50, 52, 53, 55, 65, 66, 69, 70, 75, 76, 77, 83, 84, 85, 88, 90, 91, 94, 95, 96, 97, 98, 100, 104, 109, 113, 116

INDEX

global · 15, 97
goal · 24, 26, 52, 107
grandparent · 3
gray areas · 115
Great Depression · vii, 9, 69
group dynamics · 59

H

half-birthday · 40, 41
happy · 114
harmful · 34, 36, 37
harmony · 100, 108
hesitate
  hesitates · 48
hesitation · 65
honest · 114
human need · 55
human resource · 2
hype · 71

I

ideas · viii, 37, 42, 56, 59
ideologies · 88, 89, 91

illustrate · 5, 78, 102
individuals · 6, 76, 98
industrial sectors · 3
influence · 90, 91
integrity · 13, 69, 72, 108, 117
interest · 14, 16, 78, 107
interpretation · 28

J

job rotation · 84
judgment · 36, 49
judgmental · 76

K

knowledge · 11, 65, 82, 95, 98
kudos · 35, 45, 47, 48

L

leader · vii, 69, 71, 72, 75, 84, 88, 96
leadership · 76, 78, 82, 83, 85, 91, 94, 96,

INDEX

97, 108, 116
legacy · 70
listen · 28, 31, 104
listening bias · 25
long hours · 11, 14, 75, 83
long-term · 12, 15, 18, 37, 96, 106, 114, 118
loyalty · 17, 69, 72, 84, 106

M

male · 70
Manufacturing · 116
measurement · 60, 69, 76
meeting · 22, 24, 38, 55, 57, 83, 102
meetings · 16, 72, 102, 103
method · 12, 58, 106
metrics · 59
metropolitan · 112, 118
Microsoft · 76
milestone · 47

millennials · 9, 23, 40, 89, 90, 106
mind-set · 10, 45, 108, 115
minimize · 35, 37
miscommunication · 28
mismanaged · 34, 36, 46, 51, 52
model · 55, 93
money · 56, 115, 120
motivate · 106
multigenerational · 28, 30, 100, 108, 112, 115, 118, 119, 120
multitasking · 16, 40
music · 16

N

natural · 34, 37, 100
negative · 34, 45, 51

O

onboard · 117
onboarding · 117, 118

INDEX

open-minded · 89
opinions · viii, 15, 46, 79, 106
opportunity · 10, 16, 65
organizations · 44, 82, 84, 91, 107, 108, 112, 113, 115, 118
outcomes · 12, 22, 26, 50, 54, 58, 65
owner · 28, 108

P

Palindromes · 62
palindromic · 65
panic · 17
pass judgment · 77
patterns · 59, 62, 64, 65, 66
Patterns · 62
paycheck · 106, 114, 120
peer pressure · 55
peer-to-peer · 45
perception · 23, 50, 75
Performance improvement · 46
performance review · 44
personalities · 49
philosophies · 14
physical labor · 116
physics · 65
policy · 15
politics · 84
poor management · 13, 83
popularity · 105
population · 10, 68, 78
positive approach · 104
postsecondary · 11, 18, 75, 76, 94
problematic · 42, 49, 84, 113, 116, 117, 118
problems · 48, 64, 84, 109, 117
procrastinate
procrastinate · 48
product · 10, 36, 108
production · 84
productivity · 12, 22,

INDEX

27, 29
promote · 116
prove · 14, 75, 76, 83, 86
provoke · 30, 83
purpose · 44, 114, 116, 117, 118, 120

R

reactions · 25, 35, 40
reasonable · 6, 58
relevant · 17, 96
reputation · 114, 117, 119
resentment · 9, 90
resource · 108
respect · x, xi, 58, 69, 71, 78, 83, 86, 97, 99, 100, 104, 105, 106, 108, 116
respectful · 104, 117
retirement · 41
revolving door · 82, 83
reward · 47, 117, 120
rich · xi
risk · 55, 58, 66

root cause
   root causes · 22, 23
rural · 3, 112, 118

S

SAT scores · 76
scenario · 55, 60, 104
school · 69, 75, 78, 103
self-sufficient · 14, 84
seminars · 8, 34, 46, 78, 104
senior · 82
sense of purpose · 116, 120
short-term · 37, 96, 118
skill
   skills · 23, 48, 59, 95, 97, 116
slackers · 13, 83
social media · 90
social norms · 49
social responsibility · 40, 92
social security · 15, 88
social trends · 114, 117

INDEX

societal shifts · 46
socioeconomic · 3, 6, 116
solution · 22, 23, 118
speeches · 8
stability · 10
staying late · 78
stepping-stone · 113, 114, 117
stereotyping · 25
study · viii, 5
subjective · 2, 59
substandard · 89
success · iii, viii, 10, 13, 97, 100, 108, 111, 119
suggestions · ix, xi
supervisor · 24, 26, 35, 38, 44, 49, 55, 95
synergy · 42, 108
synonymous · 105

T

target · 24, 26, 60
task · 10, 40
technology · 3, 9, 15, 16, 18, 25, 26, 61, 65, 69, 71, 72, 88, 89, 92, 96, 97, 98
timeframe · 60
tiptoe · 84
tolerance · 13, 82, 85
tragedy · 17, 89, 95
trophy · 18, 46, 50
trust · 23, 31, 35, 104, 116
turmoil · 9, 17

U

undesirable · 116
unemployed · 94
upsetting · 35
urban · 3, 15

V

valuable · 6, 55, 56
vendors · 45
vision · 111, 113, 115, 119

INDEX

W

wages · 15, 114, 117
war · 3, 17, 95
web surfing · 16
well-respected · 119
wisdom · vii, viii, xi, 48
witness
   witnessed · 35
workforce · vii, xi, 4, 10, 11, 30, 50, 65, 68, 69, 70, 74, 91, 95, 98, 108, 112, 114, 118, 120
work-life balance · 40, 70, 75
workplace · vii, viii, 2, 3, 5, 6, 8, 9, 11, 14, 15, 18, 30, 31, 34, 38, 44, 45, 58, 61, 64, 70, 71, 82, 91, 96, 97, 100, 105, 107
workplaces · 22
World War II · 9, 50, 69

Y

young
   younger · 9, 24, 27, 41, 88

ABOUT THE AUTHOR

Mr. Dennis E. Gilbert is the president of Appreciative Strategies, a human performance improvement training and consulting business. He combines his expertise in private, for-profit business management with his experience in the nonprofit educational sector to deliver outstanding results through consultation and training interventions. His extensive background in management and education is the culmination of more than thirty years of experience with both for-profit businesses and nonprofit institutions of higher learning.

Dennis helps people and businesses discover and create their futures. He is a consultant, trainer, speaker, and author who is available for worldwide engagements.

For more information visit his website:

http://DennisEGilbert.com

www.ingramcontent.com/pod-product-compliance
Lightning Source LLC
Chambersburg PA
CBHW030754180526
45163CB00003B/1013